TWENTY FUN DEVOTIONS FROM
THE LIFE OF JESUS

"It's Our Time, Dad"

20
FUN DEVOTIONS
FROM

THE LIFE OF JESUS

GREG JOHNSON

Tyndale House Publishers, Inc.
WHEATON, ILLINOIS

© 1994 by Greg Johnson
All rights reserved

Interior illustrations copyright © 1994
by Bron Smith

All Scripture quotations, unless
indicated, are from the *Holy Bible,*
New International Version®.
Copyright © 1973, 1978, 1984 by
International Bible Society. Used by
permission of Zondervan Publishing
House. All rights reserved. The "NIV"
and "New International Version"
trademarks are registered in the
United States Patent and Trademark
Office by International Bible Society.
Use of either trademark requires
permission of International Bible
Society.

Scripture verses marked TLB are taken
from *The Living Bible,* copyright ©
1971 owned by assignment by KNT
Charitable Trust. All rights reserved.

Library of Congress Catalog Card
Number 94-60985

ISBN 0-8423-1746-5

Printed in the United States of
America

99 98 97 96 95 94
7   6   5   4   3   2   1

To
Troy and Drew
that
you may know
Jesus—
and me

He will turn
the hearts
of the fathers
to their children,
and the hearts
of the children
to their fathers.
Malachi 4:6

Dads, Read This

Yes, it's tough to find the time to work on a book like this with your child, but the few total hours it will take to complete could pay dividends for years to come. Once you get started, you probably won't even have to coax or remind your child it's time to do another section. Why? Because with all of the rewards built in, they'll *want* to complete it—fast! Your child can earn points for completing various sections of each fun devotion.

As their points add up, they can cash them in for prizes—things the two of you have agreed on in advance. (See page 4 for a list of suggested prizes. Feel free to customize this list by adding things of special interest to your child and you.)

But don't go too fast through each devotion. Make sure they understand each passage. Most importantly, get ready to take a trip down memory lane. You'll find yourself recalling things about your own grade-school days you thought you'd forgotten years ago. When you're done with this book, your child will know exactly what you were like when you were his or her age!

How Long Should It Take You to Get through This Book?

There's no set amount of time. It should take ten to twenty minutes per chapter. Don't feel rushed—and don't rush. Let the lessons sink in, and help your child apply what you're learning.

Finally, though each section should relate to any child in third through sixth grade, feel free to skip a chapter or two if your kids can't relate to the subject. That will just get them to the rewards a little faster! Or, if you're finding that most of the lessons don't apply, put the book aside for a year or two until they do.

Kids, Read This

You're about to take an adventure through the life of Christ.

OK, so it probably won't be as fun as Walt Disney World. But what's fun about this adventure is that you get to take your dad with you. You can't do it alone. Along the way, as you and he complete a number of sections, you'll earn points for prizes and rewards!

The goal of this book is for you and your dad to go through selected passages from the life of Christ together, find out what they say, and especially what they mean. Your dad will be asking you some questions—some will be easy; others will require a little thought. But hey, you're up for a challenge, aren't you?

Another goal is for you to learn what your dad was like when he was your age. Does he tell you stories about when he was a kid? If he doesn't, he will now! Feel free to ask him a lot of questions on how he handled each situation. You'll learn a lot!

How fast you go through this book is up to you and your dad. When you're done with each lesson and section, mark it off in the front of the book so you can check how close you are to the next reward! You're the scorekeeper in this adventure!

The best time to remind Dad to sit down with you is probably after dinner or right before bed. You set the schedule with him so it works out best for both of you.

Are you ready? Then grab a pencil while Dad reads the rules—and then get going!

The Rules of the Game

Before you get started, Dad, let's talk about how you're supposed to be doing each lesson:

It's Alive: You or your child can read the passage. It doesn't matter who does it.

Let's Dig: Ask your child these questions. Some require thought, some are the yes-and-no variety, and some invite you to help your child find the answer. If your child gets stuck on any of them, either answer them yourself or move on to the next one. Some questions may be over the heads of second or third graders, but hopefully not too many.

Dad's Turn: This is where your child asks you the questions. The goal is for you to try to remember *stories* and *feelings* you had as a grade-schooler. If you honestly can't relate to the question or can't remember a situation, move on to the next one. If other stories come to mind that almost relate to the topic, tell them. Talking about your past is the goal.

What If . . . : It's your child's turn to answer again. You read the situation, making sure your child understands what's happening, then ask the questions. Sometimes there's one situation, sometimes more. If you're good at thinking up "What If" situations and you can think of something that may apply better to your child, then by all means use it.

Now What? This may be the most important part: application. Now's your chance to teach your child the life skill of learning how to apply passages from the Bible. Again, if what's written doesn't help your child apply the passage, think of something else that will.

Overtime Challenge: If you have enough time (and your child wants to earn bonus points), open your Bible, read the passages, and answer the questions. This should help shed some more light on the opening verses and generate more discussion.

Plant It Deep or **Pray It Up:** Some sections end with a verse to memorize, others with a prayer to pray. The memorization is optional, but again, your child will earn extra points (and more rewards) by doing it. If your time has run out, both of you can memorize it separately at a later time, then recite it before the next section to still get credit. After you're done, you can review each memorized verse to earn extra points. You don't have to be word perfect on the passages unless that's what you agree to. (A good compromise is to allow three "hints.")

Puzzles: After every five lessons there's either a crossword puzzle or a word search. The crosswords are fairly easy; the word searches could take some time. If you've got all but a couple of words, that's close enough. Just have fun doing the puzzles together.

Can This Book Be Used for Family Devotions?

Sure! If your children are close together in age—and Mom wants to be involved—go for it. All you have to do is make some decisions about how the points are kept (or perhaps not kept at all). Then when you ask the questions for kids and read the "What If" situations, try to get everyone to respond. Then when it's "Dad's turn," have Mom answer too. Not every question will apply to her, but that's OK. Just try to keep the lesson moving so the kids don't get bored.

Suggested Prize Lists

These are only suggestions for prizes. If a prize is too expensive to offer, the parent has the option to choose different prizes . . . as long as the child agrees to them, of course!

PRIZE LIST "A" (for 1,500 points or more)
• Have ice cream some weekday evening with just you and Dad.
• Rent a video and watch it together.
• Take a trip to the local library to look for some great books.
• Have lunch at a favorite fast-food spot.

- Go through old photo albums together and make a collage of pictures of just you two to put in a special wall hanging.
- Go buy a model and put it together.
- Walk to the store together to buy some junk food.
- Shoot hoops for an hour.
- Learn a new board game.
- Take a long drive.
- Make breakfast together for the whole family.
- Learn a new card game.
- Go to Dairy Queen for a Mister Misty.

- Your choice: _____
- Your choice: _____
- Your choice: _____

PRIZE LIST "B" (for 2,500 points or more)
- Buy two packs of premium sports cards.
- Go to the toy store and buy a new game to play together.
- Go to the Christian bookstore together, listen to some new tapes, and pick out the one you want.
- Go see a movie.
- Go play miniature golf together.
- Learn how to play tennis.
- Go on an all-day hike.
- Work on a project together in the garage (birdhouse, bookcase, Christmas decoration, etc.).
- Start a new collection.
- Take a trip to the zoo. (Maybe he'll take the whole family!)
- Your choice: _____
- Your choice: _____
- Your choice: _____

PRIZE LIST "C" (for 5,000 points or more)
- Go on a long bike ride and picnic with Dad.
- Dad takes you on a fifteen-dollar shopping spree at the local mall.
- Have pizza and play games at Chuck E Cheese's.

- Go bowling together once a month for three straight months.
- Take a trip to a sports card show with fifteen dollars from Dad.
- Skip church and go for a drive (just kidding).
- Make a fort or a playhouse.
- Your choice: _____
- Your choice: _____
- Your choice: _____

PRIZE LIST "D" (for 10,000 points or more)
- Your allowance gets raised by fifty cents a week for a whole year.
- Go on a one-day fishing trip with Dad.
- Have breakfast with Dad once a month for six months at a favorite breakfast spot.
- Go to a pro sports game together (getting there early enough to watch them practice).
- Go camping together for one night and day.
- Your choice: _____
- Your choice: _____
- Your choice: _____

PRIZE LIST "E" (for 15,000 points or more)
- Your allowance gets raised by one dollar a week for a whole year.
- Go on an overnight fishing trip with Dad.
- Go camping with Dad for two days.
- Buy a new Bible Nintendo game.
- Buy new tennis shoes or an outfit that you've wanted.
- Take six weeks of golf or tennis lessons together (depending on the price).
- Go snow skiing together for the day.
- Buy a new Game Boy cartridge.
- Your choice: _____
- Your choice: _____
- Your choice: _____

POINT TOTALS

Section One	Done Points	Bonus Points	Total
1. Popcorn That Won't Pop	500	_____	_____
2. Is Seeing Always Believing?	500	_____	_____
3. Throwing Rocks	500	_____	_____
4. Time for Refreshment!	500	_____	_____
5. How to Feel Good When You Make Mistakes	500	_____	_____
Add Puzzle Points			_____
Grand Total			_____
Subtract Points Redeemed			_____
Points to Be Carried Over			_____

Section Two	Done Points	Bonus Points	Total
6. Only One Road?	500	_____	_____
7. Lights, Camera, . . . Action!	500	_____	_____
8. Loving the Tough Guys	500	_____	_____
9. Do You Like Fishing?	500	_____	_____
10. How to Be Well When You're Sick	500	_____	_____
Add Puzzle Points			_____
Add Carry-over Points from Section 1			_____
Grand Total			_____
Subtract Points Redeemed			_____
Points to Be Carried Over			_____

Section Three	Done Points	Bonus Points	Total
11. Real Freedom	500	_____	_____
12. Seven Times Isn't Enough	500	_____	_____
13. Thanks Are for Giving	500	_____	_____
14. Alone, but Not Lonely	500	_____	_____
15. Do You Love the Right God?	500	_____	_____
Add Puzzle Points			_____
Add Carry-over Points from Section 2			_____
Grand Total			_____

Grand Total (from page 7)   _____
Subtract Points Redeemed   _____
Points to Be Carried Over   _____

Section Four	Done Points	Bonus Points	Total
16. The Light of Your Eyes	500	_____	_____
17. Your Soul for the World?	500	_____	_____
18. A Good Guy or a Good God?	500	_____	_____
19. The Real Bad Guy	500	_____	_____
20. How Much Are You Worth?	500	_____	_____
Add Puzzle Points			_____
Add Carry-over Points from Section 3			_____
Grand Total			_____
Subtract Points Redeemed			_____
Points to Be Carried Over			_____

Plant It Deep Review (50 points each)

Hebrews 11:6   _____
1 John 1:9, TLB   _____
John 14:6   _____
John 8:32   _____
Matthew 7:7   _____
Luke 16:11   _____
John 10:30   _____
James 4:7-8   _____

Add Review Points   _____
Add Carry-over Points from Section 4   _____
Grand Total   _____
Points Redeemed   _____

SECTION
1

Popcorn THAT WON'T Pop

IT'S ALIVE!

Jesus told them another parable: "The kingdom of heaven is like a man who sowed good seed in his field. But while everyone was sleeping, his enemy came and sowed weeds among the wheat, and went away. When the wheat sprouted and formed heads, then the weeds also appeared.

"The owner's servants came to him and said, 'Sir, didn't you sow good seed in your field? Where then did the weeds come from?'

" 'An enemy did this,' he replied.

"The servants asked him, 'Do you want us to go and pull them up?'

" 'No,' he answered, 'because while you are pulling the weeds, you may root up the wheat with them. Let both grow together until the harvest. At that time I will tell the harvesters: First collect the weeds and tie them in bundles to be burned; then gather the wheat and bring it into my barn.' " (Matt. 13:24-30)

LET'S DIG

1. Who is the man sowing the good seed? (Jesus explains this parable in Matthew 13:36-43 if you need a hint.)
2. Who is his enemy?
3. Who are the servants?
4. Most of the kids in your school are pretty good. There are a few, however, who are trouble-makers. Are they "bad seed," do they have "bad families," or are they just making "bad choices"?
5. How can you make sure you are "good seed"?

Dad's turn

- Try to remember some of the kids you didn't like in grade school. Why did those kids act mean?
- As you grew older (into high school), did your friends start making worse choices that made them bad people or better choices that made them good people? If they got worse, why was that?
- What made you start to make the better choices?

WHAT IF...

. . . Your dad popped some microwave popcorn, and there were a whole bunch of seeds that refused to pop. They're hard and, of course, have to be thrown out. Though these seeds didn't choose to be useless, they didn't do what they were made for, did they?

Though you're not a popcorn seed, pretend you are. God made you to POP! Not to sit in the bottom of the bag and be thrown away.

What do you think are some of the POPs that God made you for?

. . . There was a guy at your school who was pretty cool. One day, the teacher left the room for a couple of minutes. This guy motioned for you to come up by the teacher's desk. He whispered that you both ought to move everything around: put the papers in drawers, put the stuff in the drawers on top of the desk. This was the first time he'd ever asked you to join him in anything. If you follow along, you might be considered one of the cool guys too.

What do you feel like doing?

What do you think would happen if you gave in just this once? Would it be a onetime thing, or would there be other times he would ask you to join in on the "fun"?

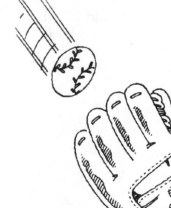

NOW *What?*

To keep from becoming "bad seed" through bad choices, you're probably going to have to say no to some of the situations your friends may want you to join in on. Write down two things that are tough for you to say no to, and talk with Dad about what to say when they come up.

1._____

2._____

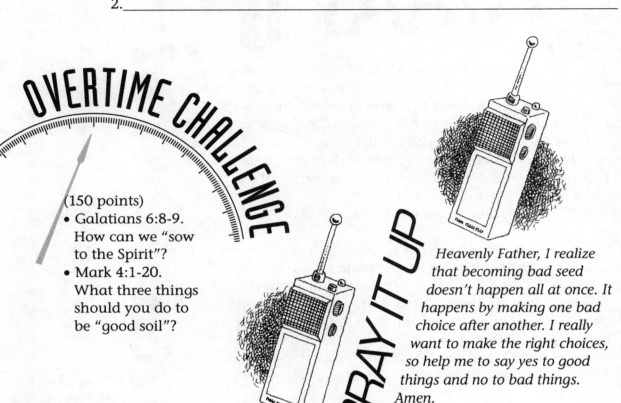

OVERTIME CHALLENGE

(150 points)
- Galatians 6:8-9. How can we "sow to the Spirit"?
- Mark 4:1-20. What three things should you do to be "good soil"?

PRAY IT UP

Heavenly Father, I realize that becoming bad seed doesn't happen all at once. It happens by making one bad choice after another. I really want to make the right choices, so help me to say yes to good things and no to bad things. Amen.

Is Seeing ALWAYS Believing?

IT'S ALIVE!

Now Thomas (called Didymus), one of the Twelve, was not with the disciples when Jesus came. So the other disciples told him, "We have seen the Lord!"

But he said to them, "Unless I see the nail marks in his hands and put my finger where the nails were, and put my hand into his side, I will not believe it."

A week later his disciples were in the house again, and Thomas was with them. Though the doors were locked, Jesus came and stood among them and said, "Peace be with you!" Then he said to Thomas, "Put your finger here; see my hands. Reach out your hand and put it into my side. Stop doubting and believe."

Thomas said to him, "My Lord and my God!"

Then Jesus told him, "Because you have seen me, you have believed; blessed are those who have not seen and yet have believed." (John 20:24-29)

LET'S DIG

1. Think of eight things that you have never seen before but that you know really exist:

- _____ - _____
- _____ - _____
- _____ - _____
- _____ - _____

2. Why is it easy to believe in those things but sometimes hard to believe that Jesus is still alive? (Dad, you answer this one too.)
3. Is it OK to doubt? Do you think God gets mad when we doubt?
4. Since we'll never see Jesus in this life, why do you think we are called more "blessed" than Thomas?
5. Do you know why God chose grace through faith in him as the way to get to heaven? (OK, I'll tell you. Everyone who ever existed can't go to church, they can't all give money, they can't all do good things, they haven't all had a Bible—but if someone tells them about Jesus, they can each believe in his grace! God's pretty smart, isn't he?)

Dad's turn

- Was there ever a time in your life when you doubted that God was really there, that he cared, and that he listened?
- What helped you get over those doubts?
- Today, when are you most tempted to doubt that God is really concerned with your life:
  1. When you get too busy?
  2. When something bad happens to you?
  3. When something bad happens to others who are close to you?
  4. When you forget to read God's Word for a long period of time?
  5. Other? _____

WHAT IF...

. . . You were allowed to actually talk face-to-face with Jesus for ten minutes. What would you ask him? Would that help you follow him the rest of your life, or would you perhaps forget about it and think that it didn't ever happen?

. . . A teacher in school said, "It really doesn't make any sense to believe in something you can't see. You should only trust what your eyes tell you, not some stories about people who died long ago . . . if they ever existed at all."

Would you have the courage to raise your hand and tell her about the eight things you listed in the first question? Or would it be just as good to talk to her after class?

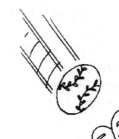

NOW *What?*

Since everyone doubts occasionally that God is really there, name three things you can do so that when you do doubt, you soon realize again that he loves you and wants to have a close daily relationship with you.

1. _____

2. _____

3. _____

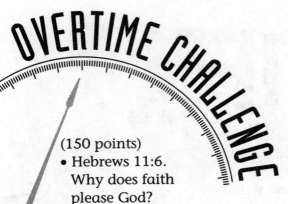

OVERTIME CHALLENGE

(150 points)
- Hebrews 11:6. Why does faith please God?
- Romans 10:17. How can reading God's Word increase our faith?
- Matthew 21:18-22. Why is having confidence in God's power so important?

PLANT IT DEEP

(150 points)
And without faith it is impossible to please God, because anyone who comes to him must believe that he exists and that he rewards those who earnestly seek him.
(Heb. 11:6)

Throwing Rocks

IT'S ALIVE!

They kept demanding an answer, so he stood up again and said, "All right, hurl the stones at her until she dies. But only he who never sinned may throw the first!" (John 8:7, TLB)

LET'S DIG

1. What do you feel like most: that you're better than everyone else or that everyone else is better than you? What makes you feel that way?
2. What makes people feel sometimes like they're better than others?
3. Have you ever gotten mad at someone for something they did that was wrong? What did you do?
4. How do you want people to treat you when you do something wrong to them?
5. What does God think of us when we do something wrong?

Dad's turn

- Explain what you think sin is. Why is it impossible to keep from sinning?
- When you were little, how did you feel after making a mistake?
- What did you need most: someone to tell you how bad you were? someone to point out what you did wrong and then offer to help you overcome it? someone you cared about to offer you forgiveness?

WHAT IF...

. . . You were playing a game with one of your friends and you caught him cheating. What would you do?

. . . You were playing a game with a couple of other friends in your room and got so mad at one of them for winning that you called him a bad name. When you looked over your shoulder, you saw that Mom had seen—and heard—the whole thing. What do you think she should do?

NOW *What?*

Write down the name of someone you know (at school, church, in the neighborhood, or on the team) who has done something bad to you: _____.

Now, imagine they just did something bad to you again. While you don't have to like what they did—and you certainly want them to stop—is it best to:

    a. scream and yell at them

    b. pretend it didn't happen

    c. tell them how you feel, but forgive them, knowing that you make mistakes too.

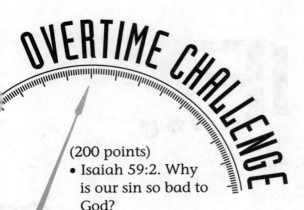

OVERTIME CHALLENGE

(200 points)
- Isaiah 59:2. Why is our sin so bad to God?
- Romans 6:23. What would happen to us if God hadn't done something about our sin?
- James 4:17. What is considered a sin according to this verse?
- 1 John 1:9. How can we get rid of our sin?

PLANT IT DEEP

(150 points)
But if we confess our sins to him, he can be depended on to forgive us and to cleanse us from every wrong. (1 John 1:9, TLB)

4

Time FOR Refreshment!

IT'S ALIVE!

"Repent, then, and turn to God, so that your sins may be wiped out, that times of refreshing may come from the Lord, and that he may send the Christ, who has been appointed for you—even Jesus." (Acts 3:19-20)

LET'S DIG

1. What are some things that are easy to say "I'm sorry" for?
2. How about things that are tough to say "I'm sorry" for?
3. Why are those two words so important?
4. When should we say we're sorry to God?
5. How do we know he hears us and forgives us? (Hint: Remember the "Plant It Deep" passage you may have memorized in chapter 2?)

Dad's turn

- When you were a kid, do you remember a time when you had to apologize to your parents for something you did? How did they respond?
- Did saying "I'm sorry" always keep you from being disciplined? Should it have?
- Was it hard for *your* dad to say he was sorry when he did something wrong? Can you remember a time when he did? How did that make you feel?

WHAT IF...

. . . You were watching TV and your mom said it was time to come set the table. When you said, "As soon as there's a commercial on," she said, "No, right now!" in kind of a loud voice. You went to the dining room, a little mad, and made a lot of noise as you set the table. She saw your attitude and told you to go to your room until you calmed down. You stomped off and slammed the door to your room behind you.

What should your mom do? What should you do?

. . . You noticed two quarters on your dad's dresser mixed in with a bunch of other change. In just a moment of greed, you took them while no one was around, knowing that you wouldn't get caught.

It's two weeks later, and your conscience has been bothering you. It's time to confess what you did.

Who did you sin most against: God or your dad? What can you do to make both relationships right again?

NOW *What?*

Having clean relationships, especially with God, feels really good. Since it seems that we're always making mistakes that are either hurting him or others, it can be difficult to keep asking for forgiveness. But we must! It will always refresh us.

Talk through with your dad the situations that come up in your home when you most need to apologize to someone else.

What are the worst ways to handle them?

What are the best ways?

What keeps you from handling those situations in the best possible way?

OVERTIME CHALLENGE

(150 points)
- Matthew 3:8. Does saying you're sorry always have to be followed by a change in behavior?
- Psalm 51:1-3. Is forgiveness given automatically, or do we have to ask for it?
- Isaiah 43:25. Does God remember our sin once we confess it to him?

PRAY IT UP

Heavenly Father, telling you—and others—"I'm sorry" isn't always easy. But I ask that when I do sin against you and others that I would be quick to ask for forgiveness. You showed us that the most important thing is a clean relationship. Help me to do what I can to keep them all clean. Amen.

5

HOW TO
Feel Good
WHEN
You Make
Mistakes

IT'S ALIVE!

When Judas, who had betrayed him, saw that Jesus was condemned, he was seized with remorse and returned the thirty silver coins to the chief priests and the elders. "I have sinned," he said, "for I have betrayed innocent blood."

"What is that to us?" they replied. "That's your responsibility."

So Judas threw the money into the temple and left. Then he went away and hanged himself. (Matthew 27:3-5)

LET'S DIG

1. When you've done something wrong, are you more likely to:
   a. admit it right away
   b. think about it for a while before saying you're sorry
   c. try to hide it as long as you can so you don't get in trouble
   d. refuse to own up to it, even when you're confronted with your wrong

2. When you do something you know is wrong, what are you most afraid of:
   a. letting your parents (or someone else you love) down
   b. discipline or punishment
   c. realizing that you make mistakes like everyone else
   d. having to ask for forgiveness

3. What is the worst thing you've done that you've had to ask forgiveness for? Was it given? How did you feel after it was all done?

4. Was Judas's response to his sadness for betraying Jesus the right thing to do?

5. What should he have done instead?

Dad's turn

- Can you remember the worst thing you did that you got caught for doing when you were in grade school?
- What did you feel like after you got caught? Were you sorry because you got caught or because what you did was wrong?
- What was the punishment? Were you glad when it was over? Did it help change you in any way?

28

WHAT IF...

... Your best friend at school started bragging about how much money he had. Though you knew his family wasn't rich, he used some of his money to buy you candy after school, so you never thought about how he got it.

After school got out one day, you came back to your classroom to talk to your teacher about an assignment. When you got in the room, you saw the teacher wasn't there, but your best friend was. He was going through her purse!

Just as you turned to leave, your teacher walked in and saw what was happening.

"So you've been the one taking money from my purse," she said, looking at your best friend. "I thought that if I left right after class, the thief would be tempted to strike again. Are you involved in this too?" she said, looking you in the eye.

After you explained you weren't, she took your best friend up to the principal's office to call his parents. He was in BIG trouble now!

What are you feeling for your best friend?

Should he be punished for what he did?

If he promised to return the money and not steal again, do you think he should be trusted in the future?

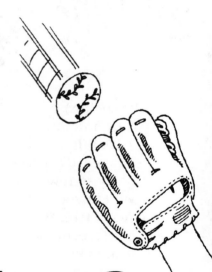

NOW *What?*

Since we all do things that are wrong, we each have a choice as to what to do after we mess up:

- We can admit our mistake right away to the person it has affected.
- We can wait awhile before admitting it.

- We can try to hide it and hope no one notices.
- We can lie when we are confronted with the truth.

The best thing to do is the first one. By waiting, hiding the truth, or lying, we set ourselves up for worse punishment when we are caught (which usually happens).

Between you and your dad, talk about what *you* can do and what *he* can do to make it easier to admit a mistake right away so you don't get in more trouble.

What will your dad have to do or change for you to feel OK about going to him after you blow it?

Is there anything right now that you need to admit to him so your relationship can start clean again?

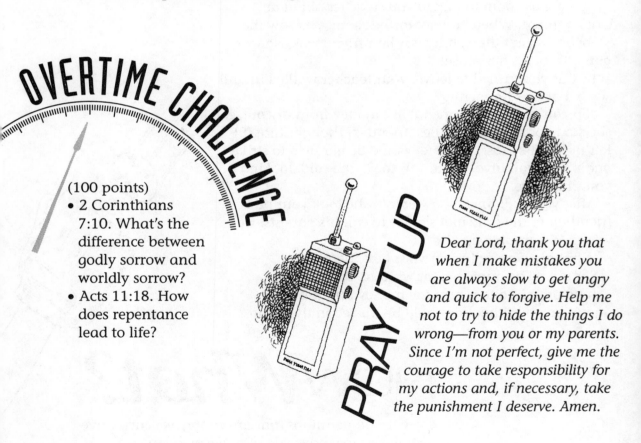

OVERTIME CHALLENGE

(100 points)
- 2 Corinthians 7:10. What's the difference between godly sorrow and worldly sorrow?
- Acts 11:18. How does repentance lead to life?

PRAY IT UP

Dear Lord, thank you that when I make mistakes you are always slow to get angry and quick to forgive. Help me not to try to hide the things I do wrong—from you or my parents. Since I'm not perfect, give me the courage to take responsibility for my actions and, if necessary, take the punishment I deserve. Amen.

BONUS PUZZLE #1

ACROSS

1 What does Jesus call us if we haven't seen and yet believe? (John 20:29)
5 What happened to the weeds that grew together with the wheat? (Matt. 13:30)
8 If we sow to please the Spirit, what do we reap? (2 wds.; Gal. 6:8)
9 What do we need to please God? (Heb. 11:6)
11 What does godly sorrow lead to? (2 Cor. 7:10)
12 Who sows the bad seed? (Matt. 13:25)

DOWN

2 ____ Thomas
3 Who betrayed Jesus? (Matt. 27:3)
4 If we repent and return to God, then times of ____ will come from the presence of the Lord. (Acts 3:19)
6 Worldly sorrow leads to ____. (2 Cor. 7:10)
7 If we sow to please our flesh, what do we reap? (Gal. 6:8)
10 What does God do if we earnestly seek him? (Heb. 11:6)

SECTION

2

Only One Road?

IT'S ALIVE!

Jesus answered, "I am the way and the truth and the life. No one comes to the Father except through me." (John 14:6)

LET'S DIG

1. What are some things people try to do to make God like them more?
2. Jesus calls himself "the way." Where does he want to take us?
3. Jesus calls himself "the truth." Does that mean that everything he says is the truth?
4. Jesus calls himself "the life." Why is it that those who don't know him don't have life? What do they have if they don't have life?
5. Jesus is like a bridge between us and God. What type of canyon does he help us get over so we can spend eternity with God?

Dad's turn

- When did you realize that there could be only one way to get to heaven?
- Talk about a couple of your acquaintances or old friends who think they can get to God through other ways besides Jesus.
- Explain the difference between *knowing about* someone and *knowing* someone.

WHAT IF...

. . . One of your friends believes that you can get to heaven just by being a good person. What would you say? (Dad, you can help on this one if it's too tough.)

. . . You have a friend who goes to church every Sunday. But when you try to ask what he believes, he says he doesn't know; he doesn't really understand what's going on in the service, so he doesn't pay attention. You then ask him if he thinks he's going to heaven. He says he hopes so, but isn't really sure.

What could you say that might help him?

NOW *What?*

Since you have probably heard *about* Jesus since you were little, does that mean you have a good relationship with God? Or does it take something more to really *know* God personally?

Have you ever crossed the bridge and let Jesus lead you to God? If not, would you like to now?

OVERTIME CHALLENGE

(100 points)
- Acts 4:12. What did Jesus do that makes his name so important as it relates to eternal life?
- 1 Timothy 2:5-6. What is a ransom? How is Jesus a ransom for us?

PLANT IT DEEP

(150 points)

Jesus answered, "I am the way and the truth and the life. No one comes to the Father except through me." (John 14:6)

7

Lights, Camera, . . . Action!

IT'S ALIVE!

For God so loved the world that he gave his one and only Son, that whoever believes in him shall not perish but have eternal life. (John 3:16)

LET'S DIG

1. *Believe* in this verse is an action word. That means it's not just something we think about—it's something we do.

   This might be kinda tough, but between the two of you, write down five things you can believe that don't require any action. (Hint: stuff like "flowers are pretty," or "baseball is fun.")

   - _____
   - _____
   - _____
   - _____
   - _____

2. Now write down five things you believe that require an action on your part to prove you really believe it.

   - _____
   - _____
   - _____
   - _____
   - _____

3. If believing in Jesus Christ is an action, what action(s) should you take to show you believe in him? Write down as many as you can think of.

- _____
- _____
- _____
- _____
- _____

Dad's turn

- Try to remember a time or two in your life when you had to put your faith in Jesus Christ to a test. That is, what you did in a certain situation was determined by what you believed about God.
- What are some areas that you still have a difficult time trusting God in?
- Why is it hard to trust God sometimes?

WHAT IF...

. . . Your dog accidentally got hit by a car and was hurt very badly. Your dad took him to the veterinarian, and she said she would do all she could to save him.

The outcome of the vet's work is totally out of your control, right? Will you trust the vet to do what's right? If the dog dies, will you be mad at the vet, God, or the driver of the car? Why?

NOW *What?*

Write down two situations you are going through that are tough to trust God in.

- _____
- _____

Have Dad pray for you right now in these areas for the coming week. Then, talk about what you can do to really trust that God can work these situations out for the best.

OVERTIME CHALLENGE

(150 points)
- John 9:35-39. How can Jesus help us not to be spiritually blind?
- 1 John 4:20. Are faith in God and loving other people somehow related?
- James 5:16. How can prayer be an action?

PRAY IT UP

Father in heaven, there are still a lot of things that are tough to trust you in down here on earth. Though I've trusted you with the most important thing—my eternal soul—some day-to-day stuff isn't as easy. Help me to believe the promises in the Bible and to trust that you are a good God who only wants what's best for me. Amen.

8

Loving
THE
Tough
Guys

IT'S ALIVE!

Love your enemies, do good to those who hate you, bless those who curse you, pray for those who mistreat you. . . . If you love those who love you, what credit is that to you? Even "sinners" love those who love them. (Luke 6:27-28, 32)

LET'S DIG

1. Why do some kids act like they hate someone?
2. Name three kids you know at school who act like they hate another student.

- _____
- _____
- _____

3. Why do some kids swear?
4. Is it hard to do good to others when they're treating you badly?
5. Why would God want us to love others even if they don't love us?

20·15·10·5·0 BC

TIME SELECTOR

Dad's turn

- Did you ever hate someone when you were in school? What did they do to make you not like them?
- Do you remember anyone in your school years that you tried to be friends with, but they just wouldn't let you? How did that make you feel?
- Think of someone who mistreated you. What did you most want to do to them:
a. do something to get even with them
b. tell them to leave you alone
c. have your dad tell their dad to tell them to leave you alone
d. pray for them and hope God would make them stop

WHAT IF...

. . . Someone from an upper grade started to swear at you or call you a bad name that rhymed with your name. Even though you asked him to stop, he wouldn't. What would you do?

. . . Your teacher asked a question one day and called on this kid next to you who's not all that smart. She gave the wrong answer, and everyone laughed because it wasn't even close to the right one. You raised your hand, not to make the other kid look stupid, but because you knew the right answer. The teacher called on you, and you gave the right answer. Now the person next to you is really mad. She whispers that she'll get you back for making her look stupid.

What would you say to her?

NOW *What?*

Think of all the kids at school that you know. Are there any that may have something against you? Name them:

- _____
- _____
- _____
- _____
- _____

First, is there anything you can do to help improve the relationship with them so they're not mad at you anymore?

Second, pray for them by name. Ask God to show them how much he loves them and to give you the chance to show them too.

OVERTIME CHALLENGE

(150 points)
- Matthew 5:44-45. Why is it so hard to pray for those who are giving you a hard time?
- Acts 7:54-60. Stephen was about to be killed, but what did he do?
- Matthew 5:9. What's the reward for being a peacemaker?

PRAY IT UP

Heavenly Father, there are times when I don't always like other people. They either get on my nerves or do something bad to me. Help me to look for ways to not lose my temper or make them mad. Since Jesus died for everyone, that must mean he cares about them a lot. Amen.

9

Do You Like Fishing?

IT'S ALIVE!

"Come, follow me," Jesus said, "and I will make you fishers of men." At once they left their nets and followed him. (Matt. 4:19-20)

LET'S DIG

1. What would you have thought if Jesus had said that to you?
2. What is he talking about?
3. Why did he ask them to fish for the souls of men?
4. How do you think they did that?
5. Do you think Jesus wants you to fish for the souls of men? Where is your ocean that you can fish in?

Dad's turn

- When you decided to follow Jesus, did you know he was going to ask you to fish for the souls of men? When did you find out that that's one thing he wants his followers to do?
- In what ways are you now fishing for the souls of men in your ocean?
- Have you and Jesus ever caught anything? Talk about what happened.

WHAT IF...

... One of your best friends didn't go to church and hadn't heard very much about Jesus or the Bible. He knew you went to church and didn't tease you.

What are some things you would say to get him interested in Jesus? How about church?

What shouldn't you say? (Dad, feel free to help with any of these questions.)

NOW *What?*

Write down the names of three people who you know aren't Christians:

- _____
- _____
- _____

First, start to pray for them every day.

Second, think of something at church you can invite them to that they would feel comfortable at.

Third, when the time is right, ask them what they know about Jesus. If they don't say much, *ask them* if you may explain to them what you know. If they're willing to listen, tell them why you're a Christian.

OVERTIME CHALLENGE

(150 points)
- Matthew 9:36-38. Could you be the answer to someone's prayer?
- Matthew 28:16-20. What do you think the word *disciple* means?
- 1 Peter 3:15. How can we become more ready to be fishers of men?

PRAY IT UP

Heavenly Father, first I want to thank you for allowing my dad to be the fisher of men in my life. Without his and Mom's teaching and example, I wouldn't know anything about you. I realize a little bit more how important it is for me to become a fisher of men. Though I don't know everything to say—and sometimes am a little afraid of what my friends would think—help me to be a good example of what a Christian is. And, if the chance ever comes up, help me to answer their questions about how to become one. Amen.

10

How
TO BE
Well
WHEN
You're
Sick

IT'S ALIVE!

While Jesus was having dinner at Matthew's house, many tax collectors and "sinners" came and ate with him and his disciples. When the Pharisees saw this, they asked his disciples, "Why does your teacher eat with tax collectors and 'sinners'?"

On hearing this, Jesus said, "It is not the healthy who need a doctor, but the sick. . . . For I have not come to call the righteous, but sinners."
(Matthew 9:10-13)

LET'S DIG

1. Dad, explain the difference between the tax collectors and Pharisees.
2. Why are the Pharisees mad that Jesus ate with tax collectors?
3. The "sick" people Jesus is referring to are those who are sinners. Who does that include today?
4. Since everyone is a sinner, no one is completely healthy. So who has Jesus come to cure?
5. How does Jesus cure us?

Dad's turn

- *Hypocrite* means "play actor." Tell your child what that means and why it's so bad—especially if you claim to be a Christian.
- Have you ever playacted your faith? Did you feel like a hypocrite?
- How have you been able to remember that you're always "sick" and in need of the Great Physician?

WHAT IF...

(I can't think of a good "What If" situation for this chapter. So you get to skip this part and go on to "Now What?" Hey, this is going to be a quick one!)

Now *What?*

When are you most tempted to be a play actor with your faith—acting like you're already good enough and don't need to hang around with Jesus?

Do you have anyone in or outside of your family you could talk to after this happens? It's important not to build a habit of thinking you don't need Jesus in your life. By having someone to tell when you're acting that way—or someone who will *tell you* when you seem to be acting that way—it will prevent you from making those playacting times a habit.

OVERTIME CHALLENGE

(150 points)
- Acts 3:1-10. What did the people think when they realized this sick man had been healed?
- Acts 16:11-15. What sickness did Lydia get healed of?

PRAY IT UP

Dear heavenly Father, first of all, help me not to be a hypocrite. Help me not to act like I'm good enough and don't need your help. Second, thank you for realizing I was sick and needed a doctor—a doctor who could cure my illness for eternity. You took away from me the penalty of my sin. Thanks. Amen.

BONUS PUZZLE #2
(1,000 points)

. . . .

```
A  N  O  I  T  C  A  P  R  L  E  Q  E
W  C  O  M  P  A  S  S  I  O  N  V  V
P  K  H  Y  W  E  R  P  N  B  I  S  S
Z  U  M  T  M  E  D  I  A  T  O  R  A
E  F  I  L  I  I  P  X  C  A  E  R  L
V  P  L  A  W  A  S  E  B  K  E  N  V
A  O  T  Y  J  G  F  S  A  L  Q  D  A
T  W  Q  R  G  F  V  M  A  Z  S  H  T
S  E  I  M  E  N  E  T  S  D  Y  A  I
U  R  A  P  U  C  I  H  H  O  E  R  O
R  F  S  D  A  O  A  Y  T  Y  B  V  N
T  U  M  E  N  B  P  N  T  U  S  E  D
S  L  P  S  A  O  E  L  I  O  R  S  S
B  H  H  E  C  S  I  U  Q  I  N  T  R
Z  I  C  R  R  U  N  N  J  S  D  Y  E
P  P  I  E  G  S  H  E  E  P  B  A  K
Q  T  C  O  H  W  E  N  M  D  R  W  R
E  C  N  O  Y  N  A  C  K  D  I  D  O
S  P  U  F  N  R  N  M  U  A  D  D  W
W  F  I  S  H  E  R  S  O  T  G  E  A
W  O  L  L  O  F  I  L  O  V  E  S  L
```

55 ~

ACTION	HARVEST	SHEEP
BRIDGE	HYPOCRITE	TRUST
CANYON	LIFE	TRUTH
COMPASSION	LOVE	WAY
EFFECTIVE	MEDIATOR	WORKERS
ENEMIES	PEACEMAKER	
FAITH	PERSECUTE	
FISHERS	POWERFUL	
FOLLOW	RELATIONSHIP	
GUILTY	SALVATION	

SECTION
3

11

Real Freedom

IT'S ALIVE!

To the Jews who had believed him, Jesus said, "If you hold to my teaching, you are really my disciples. Then you will know the truth, and the truth will set you free." (John 8:31-32)

LET'S DIG

1. If you lied to your friend and he found out about it, what would it do to your relationship?
2. If Jesus had lied, could he have ever asked people to follow his teaching?
3. How can you tell the difference between the truth and a lie? Or is it too hard to tell?
4. Do you think we can be followers of Jesus without trusting that what he says is true?

Dad's turn

- Who in your life (if anyone) has told you the truth 100 percent of the time?
- Tell the story of someone in school who told you a lie. What did you think of them when you found out?
- When you were growing up, who was most trustworthy and why?
- Did a person's motives have anything to do with whether you trusted them or not?
- How do you know God's Word is true?

WHAT IF...

. . . You'd been in school the whole year and you really liked your teacher. She had been caring and kind and had told you and your parents many times how well you were doing in school. One day in late May, she told you that she can prove that 12 + 12 = 25. Though you were pretty sure that wasn't the right answer, she'd never lied before.

What would you do or say?

NOW *What?*

Write down two situations that you are most tempted to lie to your friends about. How about your parents?

- _____

- _____

How do you feel about not telling the truth? Do you think people should trust you again after you lie to them?

One thing we have to earn in life is the trust of those who love us. Dad, what are some things your child might do in the future that would cause you not to trust him or her?

In the next five years at school, several teachers will try to tell you that God doesn't exist, that the Bible isn't true, that we are related to monkeys, and that people who go to church are weak. Do you think you would ever get to the point where you would actually believe what they say? (Even if they are nice and sincere?)

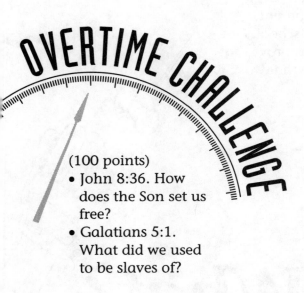

OVERTIME CHALLENGE

(100 points)
- John 8:36. How does the Son set us free?
- Galatians 5:1. What did we used to be slaves of?

PLANT IT DEEP

(150 points)
Then you will know the truth, and the truth will set you free.
(John 8:32)

12

Seven Times ISN'T Enough

IT'S ALIVE!

Then Peter came to Jesus and asked, "Lord, how many times shall I forgive my brother when he sins against me? Up to seven times?"

Jesus answered, "I tell you, not seven times, but seventy-seven times." (Matthew 18:21-22)

LET'S DIG

1. If you have a Bible close by, read the story that comes next in Matthew 18:23-35. (It's especially cool in *The Living Bible*.)
2. Why do you think Jesus is making such a big deal about forgiveness?
3. What is Jesus really saying when he says to forgive someone seventy-seven times?
4. Name five things that are easy for you to forgive.

- _____
- _____
- _____
- _____
- _____

5. Name five things that are harder for you to forgive.

- _____
- _____
- _____
- _____
- _____

20·15·10·5·0 BC
TIME SELECTOR

Dad's turn

- When you were a kid, was it easy for you to forgive others, or did you hold a grudge?
- As you got older, was it easier or harder to forgive people when they did something wrong? Why?
- Is there anything today that you consider "unforgivable"?

WHAT IF...

. . . You rode your bike to school every day. One day you didn't pull tight enough on your lock, and you walked away without realizing it wasn't locked all the way. When you went to the bike rack at the end of the day, your bike was gone!

Not only did you have to *walk* home, but you had to tell your mom that someone stole your bike because you probably didn't lock it tight enough.

About a week later, a kid comes to the door around four-thirty. Outside is a pickup with an adult in it. He says, "I'm the guy who took your bike last week. My parents found out and made me look for the owner. Some friends at school told me it was yours. I've come to return it. It's got a few spokes missing on both tires, and the seat has a tear in it. I'd pay to get it fixed, but my family doesn't have any money to pay for my stupid mistakes. They did think I should bring your bike back, though, and tell you I'm sorry. So . . . I'm sorry. Really. It was pretty dumb to take a bike. I should have known I'd get caught."

What would you say to him? (Be honest!)

Now *What?*

Think about all of the relationships in your life. Is there anyone who has done something wrong to you that you need to forgive them for? Go through this list and write down their names.

- Friends at school: _____
- Friends at church: _____
- Brothers or sisters: _____
- Mom or Dad: _____
- Relatives: _____
- Neighbors: _____

With Dad's help, figure out a way you can let them know you forgive them—even if they haven't asked for your forgiveness yet.

Putting the shoe on the other foot for a second, have you done anything to anyone that *you* need to ask forgiveness for? If so, plan with Dad how you're going to do that in the next week.

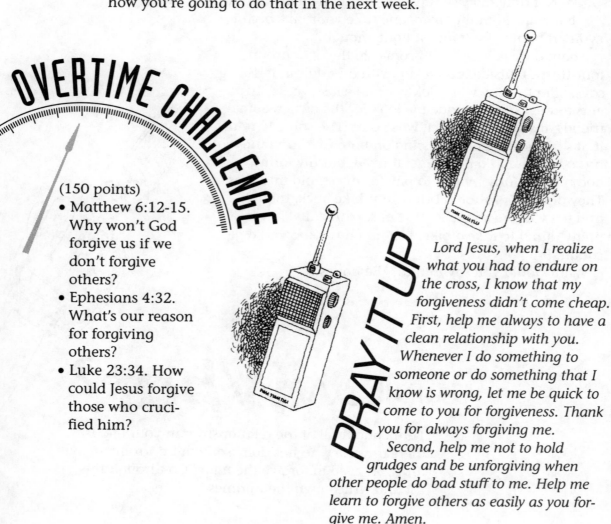

OVERTIME CHALLENGE

(150 points)
- Matthew 6:12-15. Why won't God forgive us if we don't forgive others?
- Ephesians 4:32. What's our reason for forgiving others?
- Luke 23:34. How could Jesus forgive those who crucified him?

PRAY IT UP

Lord Jesus, when I realize what you had to endure on the cross, I know that my forgiveness didn't come cheap. First, help me always to have a clean relationship with you. Whenever I do something to someone or do something that I know is wrong, let me be quick to come to you for forgiveness. Thank you for always forgiving me.

Second, help me not to hold grudges and be unforgiving when other people do bad stuff to me. Help me learn to forgive others as easily as you forgive me. Amen.

13

Thanks
ARE FOR
Giving

IT'S ALIVE!

Now on his way to Jerusalem, Jesus traveled along the border between Samaria and Galilee. As he was going into a village, ten men who had leprosy met him. They stood at a distance and called out in a loud voice, "Jesus, Master, have pity on us!"

When he saw them, he said, "Go, show yourselves to the priests." And as they went, they were cleansed.

One of them, when he saw he was healed, came back, praising God in a loud voice. He threw himself at Jesus' feet and thanked him—and he was a Samaritan.

Jesus asked, "Were not all ten cleansed? Where are the other nine? Was no one found to return and give praise to God except this foreigner?" Then he said to him, "Rise and go; your faith has made you well."
(Luke 17:11-19)

LET'S DIG

1. Have Dad explain what leprosy is (or look it up in a dictionary).
2. All ten men should have been *very* thankful for being healed of this incurable disease. Why do you think only one returned?
3. Do you ever receive something special and then forget to say thanks? Why?
4. When is it easiest to remember to say thank you? How do you feel when you do something nice for someone and they say thanks?
5. What would help you to remember to thank God and others for things you've been given?

Dad's turn

- What were you most thankful for when you were growing up? Why?
- What are the top things right now that you are most thankful for?
- How does it make you feel when you do something for someone and they don't say thanks?

WHAT IF...

... Without anyone asking you to do it, you raked the leaves off of the whole yard and no one noticed or said one word of thanks that you did it?

How would you feel? What would you do? Though we don't have to do everything for the thanks we receive, would you want to rake the leaves again?

NOW *What?*

Write down the ten things you are most thankful for.

- _____ • _____
- _____ • _____
- _____ • _____
- _____ • _____
- _____ • _____

Is there anyone you need to personally thank for those things? When can you do just that?

OVERTIME CHALLENGE

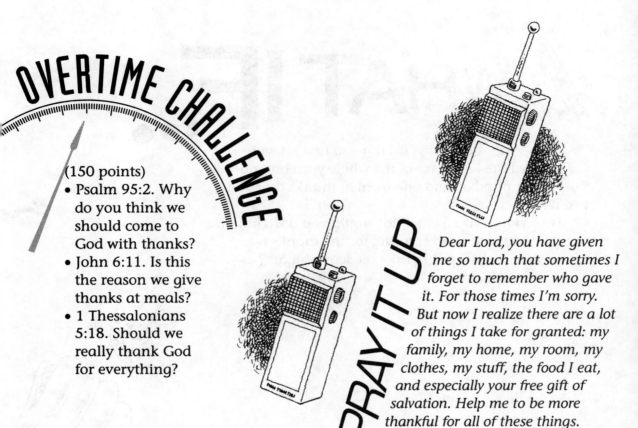

(150 points)
- Psalm 95:2. Why do you think we should come to God with thanks?
- John 6:11. Is this the reason we give thanks at meals?
- 1 Thessalonians 5:18. Should we really thank God for everything?

PRAY IT UP

Dear Lord, you have given me so much that sometimes I forget to remember who gave it. For those times I'm sorry. But now I realize there are a lot of things I take for granted: my family, my home, my room, my clothes, my stuff, the food I eat, and especially your free gift of salvation. Help me to be more thankful for all of these things. Amen.

14

Alone, BUT Not Lonely

IT'S ALIVE!

But Jesus often withdrew to lonely places and prayed. (Luke 5:16)

LET'S DIG

1. Name five things you do when you are lonely:

- _____
- _____
- _____
- _____
- _____

2. Do you ever like to go off alone by yourself sometimes? What do you like to do?
3. Why do you think Jesus needed to go away and pray?
4. When you pray, what do you pray about most?
5. Is it easy or hard to pray to God?

TIME SELECTOR
20·15·10·5·0 BC

Dad's turn

- When you were growing up, what did you like to do when you were away from others? Were you really sociable, or did you like to keep to yourself?
- Was there a time in your Christian life that you started to like spending time alone with God?
- What would you do to spend time with him?
- Were you able to stay consistent?

WHAT IF...

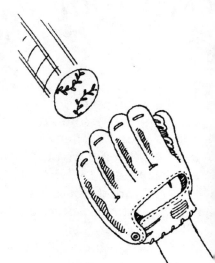

. . . You were reading your Bible alone in your room. As you were reading the words, you felt like they were speaking directly to you.

Would that be weird, or would you think that God was trying to talk to you?

. . . It was Saturday morning. You had a ten o'clock soccer game, and you got up at eight. You turned on the TV and had a bowl of cereal. It's now 8:45. You don't have to leave for another hour, and all you have to do to be ready is get dressed.

Would you take five or ten minutes and spend time with God, or would you watch more TV?

Why is this such a tough decision to make?

Do you think someone wants to prevent you from spending time with God?

NOW *What?*

Have you ever tried to spend time with God *every* day? If Jesus went off by himself to spend time with his Father, so must we. But it's tough sometimes trying to find time to do it. Here's a solution that might work.

What are two things you do in the same order every day? Is it putting your clothes on and then eating breakfast? Is it brushing your teeth and watching TV before heading off to school?

Between you and Dad, come up with a time each day that you can spend five minutes with God. Try to put it *between* two things you do each day so it will be easy to remember.

Now, help Dad do the same thing, if he doesn't already have a scheduled time with God.

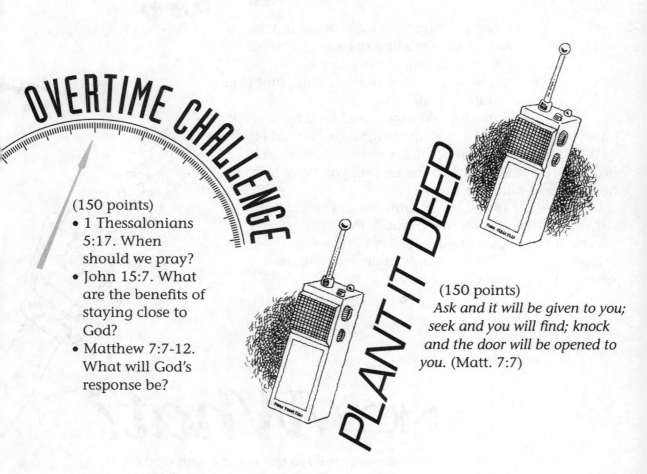

OVERTIME CHALLENGE

(150 points)
- 1 Thessalonians 5:17. When should we pray?
- John 15:7. What are the benefits of staying close to God?
- Matthew 7:7-12. What will God's response be?

PLANT IT DEEP

(150 points)
Ask and it will be given to you; seek and you will find; knock and the door will be opened to you. (Matt. 7:7)

15

Do You Love THE Right God?

IT'S ALIVE!

No one can serve two masters. Either he will hate the one and love the other, or he will be devoted to the one and despise the other. You cannot serve both God and Money. (Matthew 6:24)

LET'S DIG

1. Besides sleeping and going to school, name the three things that you spend most of your time on:

- _____
- _____
- _____

2. Do you feel like you spend too much time on those three?
3. What do you think the word *devoted* means? (Look in the dictionary if you need to.)
4. Is it easier to like things you can see than it is to like God, whom you can't see?
5. Why do you think God wants us to be devoted to him instead of money or things?

20·15·10·5·0 BC
TIME SELECTOR

Dad's turn

- What do you spend most of your time on (outside of work and sleeping)?
- Describe a recent time when you valued other things more than God.
- How do you try to show God that you are more devoted to him than anything else?

WHAT IF...

. . . For your birthday you were given more than one hundred dollars in cash from all of your friends and relatives. It was more money than you'd ever been given in your life. Would you do anything with that money to show you are more devoted to God than all that cash? What would it be?

. . . You had a collection—of sports cards, stamps, magazines, comic books, dolls, or whatever—that you spent a lot of time with. In fact, when you got up in the morning and when you arrived home from school, the first thing you did was give your attention to it. Your mom mentions that she thinks the collection is becoming too important.

What would you tell her?

NOW *What?*

Think of all of the things you have or do that take up time (hobbies, friends, entertainment choices, talking on the phone, sports, etc.). Make a list of them below, and write down how much time per week you spend on each of them.

- _____   • _____
- _____   • _____
- _____   • _____
- _____   • _____

Between you and Dad, ask yourself if you are spending too much time on any of these, or if any are so important that you're forgetting about God.

We need to keep things in their right place. If something becomes so important that you're neglecting time with your family or God, you may need to do some rearranging. We should be devoted only to God, not the things he's given us to enjoy.

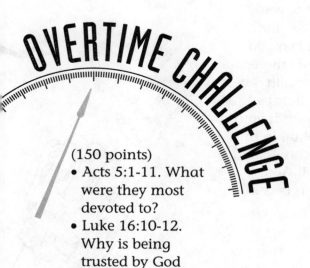

OVERTIME CHALLENGE

(150 points)
- Acts 5:1-11. What were they most devoted to?
- Luke 16:10-12. Why is being trusted by God so important?

PLANT IT DEEP

(150 points)
So if you have not been trustworthy in handling worldly wealth, who will trust you with true riches? (Luke 16:11)

BONUS PUZZLE #3
(750 points)

ACROSS

2 Jesus often ___ to lonely places. (Luke 5:16)
5 Be compassionate and ___. (Eph. 4:32)
6 If we hold to Jesus' teaching, we are his ___. (John 8:31)
7 When you don't forgive someone, it's called holding a ___.
9 We should give thanks in all ___. (1 Thess. 5:18)
10 What made the leper well? (Luke 17:19)
11 What did Jesus say we should do more than seventy-seven times?
13 "If the Son sets you ___ . . . " (John 8:36)

DOWN

1 "Then you will know the ___." (John 8:32)
3 Let us come before him with ___. (Ps. 95:2)
4 "You cannot serve God and ___." (Matt. 6:24)
8 For everyone who asks ___. (Matt. 7:8)
10 If we stand ___, then we won't be a slave again. (Gal. 5:1)
12 Be trustworthy in worldly wealth so you can be trusted with true ___. (Luke 16:11)

SECTION
4

16

THE Light OF Your Eyes

IT'S ALIVE!

Your eye is the lamp of your body. When your eyes are good, your whole body also is full of light. But when they are bad, your body also is full of darkness. See to it, then, that the light within you is not darkness. (Luke 11:34-35)

LET'S DIG

1. Name five things you can look at that aren't good for you:

   - _____
   - _____
   - _____
   - _____
   - _____

2. Looking at things sometimes makes us want what we see. This is called being greedy or "coveting." (Look that word up in a dictionary if neither of you understands what it means.)
3. Why is being greedy, or coveting, so bad?
4. How can you learn to be satisfied with what you have and not always want what you see?
5. How do you think it could hurt you if you wanted everything you saw?

84

Dad's turn

- When you were a kid, what were some things you really wanted but couldn't have? Why couldn't you have them?
- Now that you have kids of your own, why don't you try to give them everything they want?
- What are some things you would like right now but for one reason or another can't have? How do you feel about that?

WHAT IF...

. . . You were at Target, walking around in the toy section. Suddenly, you spied this toy that was out of its package, lying in the aisle. The toy was small enough to fit into your pocket. No one was around, so it would be easy to take. Besides, a store employee will probably pick it up and throw it away anyway.

What would be your thoughts?

Who would know that you took the toy?

. . . While over at your friend's house, you noticed he's got a stereo, Nintendo, TV, and a VCR in his bedroom! Whoa! You know that if your parents were going to buy you stuff like that, they'd have to work twenty more hours every week.

When you walked into your room back at home, you were reminded that all you have is a small cassette player with a radio.

Would you rather have the extra "toys," or would you rather have more time with your parents?

Who is better off, you or your friend?

NOW *What?*

Write down all of the things you can think of that you need in order to survive:

- _____
- _____
- _____
- _____
- _____
- _____

Now write down all of the extra things you have in your house or your room that some kids in your school may not have.

- _____
- _____
- _____
- _____

- _____
- _____
- _____
- _____

Which is better: to be thankful for what you have, or to worry about what you don't have compared to a few others?

With Dad right now, pray that you both would be more content with what you have and not worry about what you don't have. (You can use the prayer below, if you want.)

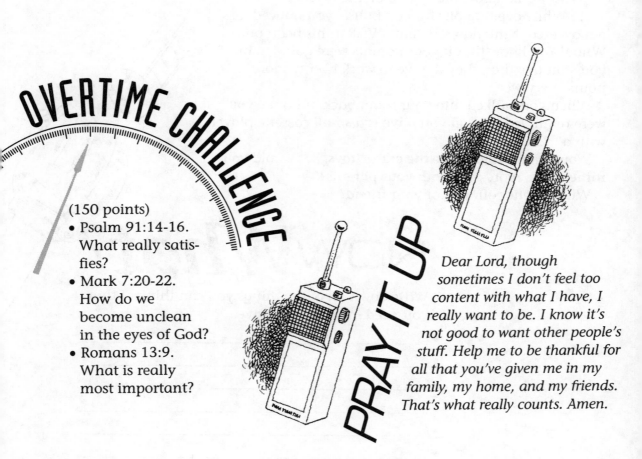

OVERTIME CHALLENGE

(150 points)
- Psalm 91:14-16. What really satisfies?
- Mark 7:20-22. How do we become unclean in the eyes of God?
- Romans 13:9. What is really most important?

PRAY IT UP

Dear Lord, though sometimes I don't feel too content with what I have, I really want to be. I know it's not good to want other people's stuff. Help me to be thankful for all that you've given me in my family, my home, and my friends. That's what really counts. Amen.

17

Your Soul FOR THE World?

IT'S ALIVE!

What good is it for a man to gain the whole world, yet forfeit his soul? Or what can a man give in exchange for his soul? (Mark 8:36-37)

LET'S DIG

1. What is our body made of? Name all the different components you can think of (Dad, you can help).

- _____
- _____
- _____
- _____
- _____

2. From this passage, how do we know for sure we have a soul?
3. Why is our soul so important to Jesus?
4. Is there anything we can own that will give our soul more value in the next life?
5. If our soul is still scarred by the penalty of sin when we die, would it matter if we were the richest person on earth?

TIME SELECTOR

20·15·10·5·0 BC

Dad's turn

- When surgeons operate on the brain, many admit they sense there is something more there than flesh and blood. Do you remember when you first realized there was more to your life than just what you can see?
- In your opinion, why do some people believe they don't have a soul—something God-given that lasts forever?
- Many Christians believe the soul is what houses our personality; it's what makes each of us different, so that when we get to heaven, we will still be unique individuals. What do you think?

WHAT IF...

... You talked to someone at school who didn't believe in God and Jesus or heaven and hell. They said that when you die, that's it.

Does this person know for 100 percent pure fact that this is true? Or are they just hoping it's true so they won't have to think about having someone they can't see "try to run their life"?

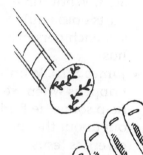

Now *What?*

Very few people, teachers, or books—besides Christians and the Bible—say that man has a soul or a spirit that will actually live forever. Because most people only choose to believe what they see and don't trust God (because they've never met him), they might think you're stupid or foolish for believing that.

Talk with Dad about what to say if someone does make fun of you someday for trusting what God says in the Bible about us having a soul that will live forever.

OVERTIME CHALLENGE

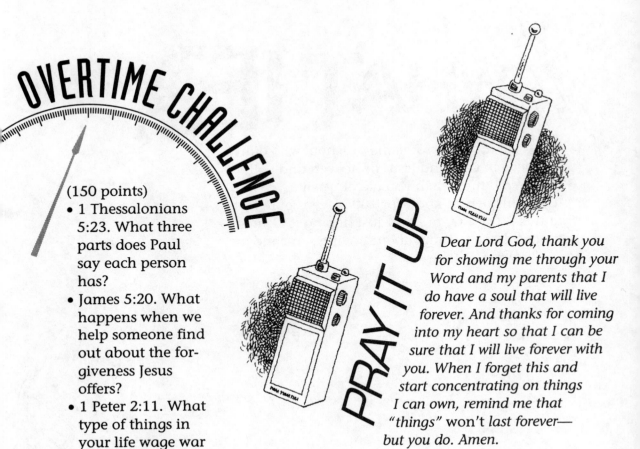

(150 points)
- 1 Thessalonians 5:23. What three parts does Paul say each person has?
- James 5:20. What happens when we help someone find out about the forgiveness Jesus offers?
- 1 Peter 2:11. What type of things in your life wage war against your soul?

PRAY IT UP

Dear Lord God, thank you for showing me through your Word and my parents that I do have a soul that will live forever. And thanks for coming into my heart so that I can be sure that I will live forever with you. When I forget this and start concentrating on things I can own, remind me that "things" won't last forever— but you do. Amen.

18

A Good Guy OR A Good God?

IT'S ALIVE!

When the men came to Jesus, they said, "John the Baptist sent us to you to ask, 'Are you the one who was to come, or should we expect someone else?'"

At that very time Jesus cured many who had diseases, sicknesses and evil spirits, and gave sight to many who were blind. So he replied to the messengers, "Go back and report to John what you have seen and heard: The blind receive sight, the lame walk, those who have leprosy are cured, the deaf hear, the dead are raised, and the good news is preached to the poor." (Luke 7:20-22)

LET'S DIG

1. Dad, explain who John the Baptist was. Who were all the people looking for?
2. If Jesus was just a regular guy, do you think he could have done all of those miraculous things?
3. Since Jesus did so many good things, isn't it OK to believe that he was just a good person and not really God?
4. Is it hard for you to believe that Jesus did all these things since you didn't actually see him do them? Or is it easy to believe what the Bible says Jesus did?
5. What do you think the "good news" was that Jesus preached to the poor?

Dad's turn

- When you first heard about Jesus, did you wonder if he was really the one you should follow, or was he the clear choice over other options? (What were the other options, if any?)
- Has Jesus ever done any "miraculous" things in your life? What is the biggest miracle?
- From your experience, why do you think some people don't believe the "Good News" is actually good news?

WHAT IF...

. . . You were eating lunch one day in the cafeteria and you found out one of your classmates goes to a different type of church than you do. They have other books they follow besides the Bible. And though they believe that Jesus was God's Son—and that his words are important—they also believe the leader of their church spoke for God too.

Since you believe that Jesus is the only way to God, what she's saying really doesn't make that much sense. What would you do or say to explain your beliefs?

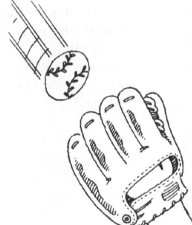

NOW *What?*

Beginning today, write down all of the miracles God has done in your life and the life of your family. You can start with God's gift of salvation, but also include as many answered prayers as you can recall.

Why should you make a list of things God has done for you? So that when other people (or Satan) try to convince you God really isn't alive or isn't involved in his kids' lives, you can go back to the list and realize how much he cares for you.

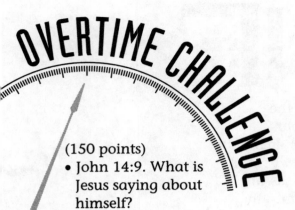

OVERTIME CHALLENGE

(150 points)
- John 14:9. What is Jesus saying about himself?
- Hebrews 1:1-3. What does this say about who Jesus is?
- John 10:30. Again, what is Jesus saying about himself?

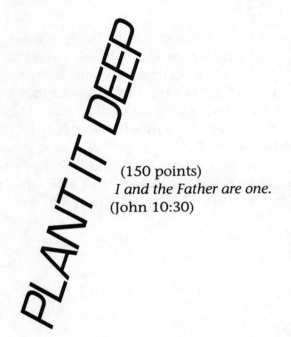

PLANT IT DEEP

(150 points)
I and the Father are one.
(John 10:30)

19

The Real Bad Guy

IT'S ALIVE!

Do not be afraid of those who kill the body but cannot kill the soul. Rather, be afraid of the One who can destroy both soul and body in hell.
(Matthew 10:28)

LET'S DIG

1. Name four things you are really afraid of:

- _____
- _____
- _____
- _____

2. Have you ever feared for your life? (How about you, Dad? Was there ever a time when you felt your life was threatened?) Try to describe that kind of fear.
3. What does the word *destroy* mean to you?
4. Why do you think people—even Christians—aren't that afraid of Satan today?
5. Christians don't need to fear Satan, but since Jesus called him "the prince of this world," we do need to recognize that he exists and is powerful. How can we be more aware of the bad things he is trying to do in our life without dwelling on him?

Dad's turn

- When did you first know that there was a darker power who hated you and wanted to do everything he could to keep you away from believing and following Christ?
- Confidence and trust in Christ's power can overcome Satan's influence. When did you gain that confidence?
- How does Satan try to influence or tempt you today?

WHAT IF...

The "Now What?" section below has a "What If" situation in it already. Skip down to it, and see if Satan has been trying to influence you without you really knowing it.

NOW *What?*

Satan knows better than to show all of his ugliness all at once. If he did that, he knows that everyone would reject him right away. Instead, he patiently tries to move people one step at a time away from the truth.

A good example might be lying. He whispers in our ear: "It's harmless to tell fibs to friends, isn't it?" So, perhaps we do. Later, he says the same thing about not telling the whole truth to a brother or sister. Then a teacher. Sooner or later, one of your parents. Some kids, if they believe that fibs aren't actually lies, will not even feel guilty about telling them because they've been doing it for so long.

Do you have one area in your life that maybe you've allowed Satan to convince you isn't so bad? It could be using bad language, stealing, lying, laziness, not paying attention to God's Word. You decide.

With Dad's help, how can you start over and learn to realize that one small sin leads to another?

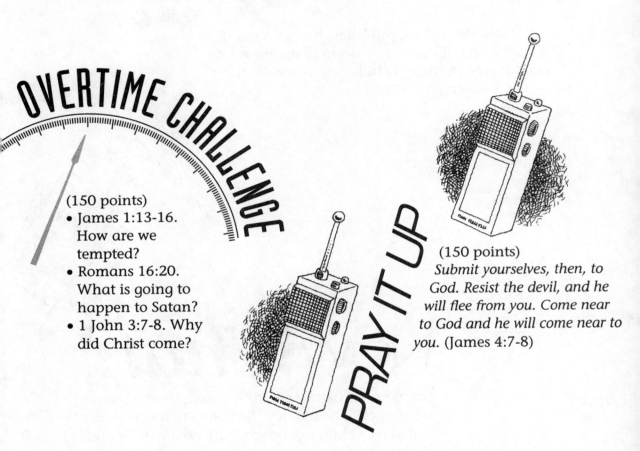

OVERTIME CHALLENGE

(150 points)
- James 1:13-16. How are we tempted?
- Romans 16:20. What is going to happen to Satan?
- 1 John 3:7-8. Why did Christ come?

PRAY IT UP

(150 points)
Submit yourselves, then, to God. Resist the devil, and he will flee from you. Come near to God and he will come near to you. (James 4:7-8)

20

How Much Are You Worth?

IT'S ALIVE!

Are not five sparrows sold for two pennies? Yet not one of them is forgotten by God. Indeed, the very hairs of your head are all numbered. Don't be afraid; you are worth more than many sparrows. (Luke 12:6-7)

LET'S DIG

1. Have you ever wondered how God can keep track of everything?
2. Why do you think we are worth so much to God?
3. It makes sense that if you had the power to create something, you have the power to take care of it. What have you made with your own hands that you are really proud of? Did you try to take care of it as best you could?
4. Do you sometimes wonder if God can really take care of all of the things that you're concerned about: school, sports, friends, family, and your future?
5. How has/does God show(n) you that you are a valuable person and that he cares about what you care about?

Dad's turn

- Do you ever remember feeling worthless as a kid? Why do you think that was?
- Did you grow up hearing how valuable you are to God? If you didn't, what *did* you hear from people about yourself?
- These days, when are you most tempted to think that no one cares or that you're worthless?

WHAT IF...

... You were playing baseball in a summer league game. It was the last inning, your team was up by one run, and you were playing center field. The first batter up hit a fly ball straight to you—but you dropped it, and the runner ended up on second base. The next batter up hit a hard ground ball right up the middle. You charged it, but it went between your legs and rolled another thirty feet. By the time you got to it, the guy on second had scored and the batter was heading for third. You picked the ball up and threw it to third—but it went over the third baseman's head and out of play. The run scored, and you lost the game.

Afterward, three of your teammates got on your case about making three errors in the last inning to lose the game. They even started saying stuff to each other like, "Having *no* center fielder would be better than the one we have!"

Dad said, "Don't worry about it. It's just one game. There'll be others" (like all good dads would say). But you still felt lousy.

Who's right, your teammates or your dad? Why?

Should you think that you're worthless over what someone says or worthwhile because of who you are?

NOW *What?*

Write down three things or situations in your life that make you feel worthless:

- _____
- _____
- _____

What one fact should you keep in mind after each of these things happens so you can *realize the truth* instead of *react to the situation?*

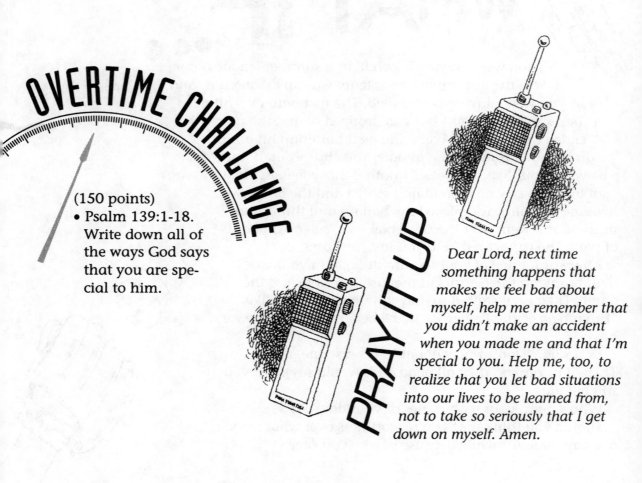

OVERTIME CHALLENGE

(150 points)
• Psalm 139:1-18. Write down all of the ways God says that you are special to him.

PRAY IT UP

Dear Lord, next time something happens that makes me feel bad about myself, help me remember that you didn't make an accident when you made me and that I'm special to you. Help me, too, to realize that you let bad situations into our lives to be learned from, not to take so seriously that I get down on myself. Amen.

BONUS PUZZLE #4
(1,000 points)

. . . .

```
A  S  P  O  I  L  E  D  E  R  U  C  R  I  W
H  S  W  O  R  R  A  P  S  J  O  A  T  A  O
R  T  A  S  T  R  A  Y  T  V  I  I  R  H  N
A  E  X  C  H  A  N  G  E  S  E  V  I  L  D
D  A  P  T  E  R  W  T  E  F  I  N  J  S  E
I  L  R  R  Q  U  I  D  R  S  O  S  F  L  R
A  I  E  A  E  N  T  O  H  S  X  L  E  F  F
N  N  A  Q  G  S  F  I  U  E  I  I  O  R  U
C  G  C  R  A  S  E  K  N  N  T  G  E  S  L
E  N  H  E  A  R  A  N  T  K  Z  H  W  U  L
I  O  E  S  P  I  R  I  T  R  T  T  A  N  Y
Y  A  D  S  G  H  F  B  M  A  A  H  L  C  O
D  T  H  G  I  S  U  Q  F  D  T  E  K  L  L
O  M  I  R  A  C  L  E  S  E  Z  I  H  E  U
B  E  C  N  E  U  L  F  N  I  N  J  O  A  O
M  A  J  E  S  T  Y  X  M  K  N  O  W  N  S
```

ASTRAY	INFLUENCE	SIGHT
BODY	KNIT	SOUL
COVETING	KNOWN	SPARROWS
CURED	LIGHT	SPIRIT
DARKNESS	MAJESTY	SPOILED
EVIL	MIRACLES	STEALING
EXCHANGE	ONE	UNCLEAN
FATHER	PREACHED	WALK
FEARFULLY	RADIANCE	WAR
FORFEIT	RAISED	WONDERFULLY
HEAR	REPRESENTATION	
HEART	RESIST	

. . . .

104

```
            B L E S S E D
                          O
  J       R               U
B U R N E D               B T
  D       E       D       I
  A       F       E       N
  S       R   D   A       G
          E T E R N A L L I F E
          S   S   T
F A I T H  H   T   H
          I   R
  R       N   U
  E       G   C
  W           T
  A           I
S A L V A T I O N
  R           O
  D       E N E M Y
```

Bonus Puzzle #2—Answers to word search, page 55

(1,000 points)

. . . .

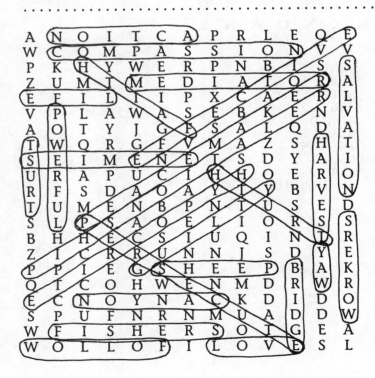

Bonus Puzzle #3—Answers to crossword puzzle, page 79

```
            T
W I T H D R E W
    H       U
    A       T
K I N D     H
    K
D I S C I P L E S    G R U D G E        M
    G                    E              O
    I                                   N
    C I R C U M S T A N C E S           E
    V                    E              Y
F A I T H       F O R G I V E
I   N           R       V
R   G           I       E
M               C       S
                H
        F R E E S
                S
```

Bonus Puzzle #4—Answers to word search, page 103
(1,000 points)

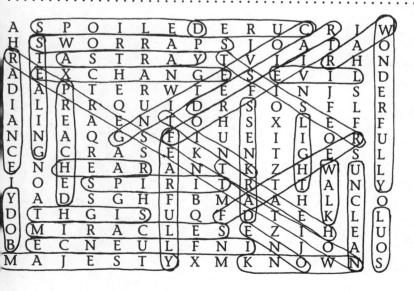

I'd like to hear from you!

1. If you have a "What If" situation that applies better to a certain chapter, write it out and send it.

2. If you thought up different (better?) prizes, write and tell me.

3. Was the book too long? too short? just right? How long did it take you to do this book with your child(ren)? How old were they? Were any chapters too tough? too easy? Send a brief evaluation.

Send your responses to any of these questions to:

Greg Johnson
c/o Tyndale House Publishers
P.O. Box 80
Wheaton, IL 60189-0080